I0748472

ISBN: 9780995651654
Published by Angelis Publications
www.angelispublications.com
Cover Design Angie J Anderson

Guest Book to Commemorate

Guests

Guests

Guests

Guests

Guests

Guests

Guests

Guests

Guests

Guests

Guests

Guests

Guests

Guests

Guests

Guests

Guests

Guests

Guests

Guests

Guests

Guests

Guests

Guests

Guests

Guests

Guests

Guests

Guests

Guests

Guests

Guests

Guests

Guests

Guests

Guests

Guests

Guests

Guests

Guests

Guests

Guests

Guests

Guests

Guests

Guests

Guests

Guests

Guests

Guests

Guests

Guests

Guests

Guests

Guests

Guests

Guests

Guests

Guests

Guests

Guests

Guests

Guests

Guests

Guests

Guests

Guests

Guests

Guests

Guests

Guests

Guests

Guests

Guests

Guests

Guests

Guests

Guests

Guests

Guests

Guests

Guests

Guests

Guests

Guests

Guests

Guests

Guests

Guests

Guests

Guests

Guests

Guests

Guests

Guests

www.ingramcontent.com/pod-product-compliance
Lightning Source LLC
Chambersburg PA
CBHW081126300726
48982CB00005B/867